A QUICK GUIDE TO

Reviving Disengaged Writers

5–8

Other Books in the Workshop Help Desk Series

*A Quick Guide to
Reaching Struggling Writers, K–5*
M. COLLEEN CRUZ

*A Quick Guide to
Teaching Persuasive Writing, K–2*
SARAH PICARD TAYLOR

*A Quick Guide to
Making Your Teaching Stick, K–5*
SHANNA SCHWARTZ

*A Quick Guide to
Boosting English Acquisition in Choice Time, K–2*
ALISON PORCELLI AND CHERYL TYLER

*A Quick Guide to
Teaching Second-Grade Writers with Units of Study*
LUCY CALKINS

*A Quick Guide to
Teaching Reading Through Fantasy Novels, 5–8*
MARY EHRENWORTH

For more information about these and other titles,
visit www.firsthand.heinemann.com.

A QUICK GUIDE TO
Reviving Disengaged Writers
5–8

CHRISTOPHER LEHMAN

Workshop Help Desk Series
Edited by Lucy Calkins
with the Reading and Writing Project

DEDICATED TO TEACHERS™
HEINEMANN
Portsmouth, NH

An imprint of Heinemann
361 Hanover Street
Portsmouth, NH 03801–3912
www.heinemann.com

Offices and agents throughout the world

Library of Congress Cataloging-in-Publication Data
Lehman, Christopher.
  A quick guide to reviving disengaged writers, 5–8 / Christopher Lehman.
      p. cm. — (Workshop help desk series)
  Includes bibliographical references.
  ISBN 13: 978-0-325-04280-0
  ISBN 10: 0-325-04280-2
  1. English language—Composition and exercises—Study and teaching
(Elementary). 2. English language—Composition and exercises—Study and
teaching (Middle school). I. Title.
  LB1576.L376 2011
  372.62′3—dc23   2011020225

SERIES EDITOR: *Lucy Calkins and the Reading and Writing Project*
EDITORS: *Kate Montgomery and Teva Blair*
PRODUCTION: *Victoria Merecki*
COVER DESIGN: *Monica Crigler and Jenny Jensen Greenleaf*
FRONT COVER PHOTO: *Peter Cunningham*
BACK COVER PHOTO: *Yesenia Garcia*
INTERIOR DESIGN: *Jenny Jensen Greenleaf*
COMPOSITION: *House of Equations, Inc.*
MANUFACTURING: *Veronica Bennett*

Printed in the United States of America on acid-free paper
15 14 13 12 11 VP 1 2 3 4 5

To Mom, Dad, and Amy.
Always engaging.

C O N T E N T S

A C K N O W L E D G M E N T S

My deepest appreciation to Lucy Calkins for her un-
yielding belief in children and the educators who
serve them; my gratitude for her mentoring and encourage-
ment could never be put into precise enough words. Additionally, to Mary Ehrenworth, Laurie Pessah, Kathleen Tolan,
and Kathy Neville for your leadership and care.

To all of my colleagues at the Reading and Writing Project,
your ideas and inspiration are the DNA of everything I do; in-
cluding Kate Roberts, Maggie Beattie, Audra Robb, Janet
Steinberg, Garret Kyle, Jerry Maraia, Cia Pinkerton, Elisa
Zonana, Stacey Fell-Eisenkraft, Jen Serravallo, and Emily
DeLiddo.

My thanks to Kate Montgomery; your wisdom is un-
matched. Your careful insight brought this title into being and
your care for this profession continues to inspire. Also, thanks
to the members of the Heinemann team: you are a pleasure to
create with.

My endless awe for the teachers and administrators from
around the world who I have been lucky enough to study
alongside and whose work are woven throughout these pages;
your students are lucky to have you; including Sharon, Ron,
Barbara, and staff of IS 230; Zoi, Barbara, Brenda, and staff of
JHS 67; my friends at the Queen Rania Teacher Academy,
Jordan; Elaine, Cynthia, Nora, and staff in Livingston, NJ; Steve

and staff in Washington Township, NJ; everyone in Union County Middle Schools, NC; and the inspiring staff of Rancho Santa Fe, CA.

Finally, and most important, to Yesenia, Tahlya, and Marcos for your time, belief, and love—thank you.

I know I do not need to tell you this: our students are masters of disengagement. They have millions of ways of checking out, though the reasons why are somewhat more elusive, and what to do about it is an even greater challenge. There is that student who every time writing workshop begins suddenly asks to use the bathroom. "But lunch just ended," you say to her. "I know, but I really have to go," she says as she jumps up to the door. Her notebook has day after day of half-written pages. Or the class that after a few productive minutes of writing suddenly erupts into conversation. You walk the room, shooting disapproving glances and making mysterious marks on a clipboard, "Jeremy, Mario, that's a minus point. Get back to writing, stop talking." The trick works for today, but every day you find yourself becoming more and more the writing police, not the writing teacher.

I am sure you find, too, that it is not just students you might refer to as "struggling" who become disengaged in your writing workshop. Even your most adept writers either seem to shut down or, even more commonly, switch to a mindless autopilot that leads to task completion but not writing growth. Therefore, I argue that disengagement is an issue broader than simply *struggling* writers; instead it is about all middle school writers who lose steam at times and need a jump start.

This book is written for you, to help you create the kind of writing workshop in which all of your students can thrive, despite some of their best efforts not to. While this book could be for any classroom, and probably some of these strategies could work across even other subject areas, it is written with the general assumption that you are supporting your students' learning in a workshop format, where they have time to write for long periods of time, on subjects of their own choosing, with your guidance, modeling, and conversations. What I make no assumptions about is that it is an easy thing. Instead, I am quite certain that whether you are a first-year teacher or someone who has been studying workshop for twenty-five years, you have moments—probably several a month—where you scratch your head and say, "Okay, now what?" Because you are making a commitment to student-centered, not program-centered, instruction, your teaching is constantly evolving with your changing clientele. So consider this book as part of that figuring out you do all the time, a conversation we can have together about trying to tackle one faction of your writing workshop: your disengaged writers.

The book is also written with the unique challenges of a middle school classroom in mind, although the ideas here can be used with students both older and younger. Middle school grade levels are quite different from district to district across states, some consisting of fifth through eighth grade, others only seventh and eighth grade (like the one I attended), and still others contained within a larger elementary or high school. When I use the term "middle school" in this book, I am referring to our ever-changing, always interesting young adults from fifth through eighth grade.

The chapters are organized with the intention of being a quick resource, one you can reference over time. The first four chapters are intended to help you consider ways you might counteract certain troubles brewing in your room, like overly talkative classes or students who constantly need your approval. The strategies presented are ones developed with hundreds of teachers across the country faced with disengaged writers. This book contains some of the most effective fixes from the many, many "uh-ohs" I have faced while standing alongside many of you. The last chapter then suggests an inquiry process you could follow to support you in developing your own approaches to reviving the disengaged writers in your room.

I hope you will think of this book as a companion to others in this "Quick Guide" series, as well as to the *Units of Study* books developed by Lucy Calkins and the Teachers College Reading and Writing Project community. While this title addresses middle school writers' disengagement, you might also look to M. Colleen Cruz's *A Quick Guide to Reaching Struggling Writers, K–5*, which gives practical tips for students who specifically struggle with writing in the elementary grades. Tips in both this book and M. Colleen's could realistically traverse across grade levels—as our students' abilities are bound not by a grade number but instead by their own developmental needs. Therefore, you might consider looking between them, and at other titles, as you shape your writing workshop.

So, grab your notebook, a pen, maybe some colleagues, and let's go into your classroom together.

A QUICK GUIDE TO

Reviving Disengaged Writers

5–8

CHAPTER ONE

Writers Who Are Nearly Allergic to the Writing Process

This chapter will help you to:

- ▶ Make their efforts measurable: teach them to create quantitative goals
- ▶ Reframe revision: make it an act of experimentation, not correction
- ▶ Connect them with texts they love: help them apprentice themselves to books they admire

Case Study

During a day in a middle school outside of Oakland, California, some teachers and I sat down next to two writers. Earlier in the period I taught a fiction revision lesson to the class and then left them to work on their writing. Many of their classmates were busily writing their drafts, but two sat mostly uncertain from the start, reading and rereading, instead of using their pencils to do much of anything. The teacher said that they were some of the stronger writers in the room, and one in particular loved to write. Though, he added, it was not uncommon to find them stuck with "what to do next."

The girls sat at the table; a group of teachers and I gathered around. I wanted to get in good with them, so I started with a compliment and then moved to figuring out what was going on. "It looks like you wrote tons on your draft. It's so impressive how you did not hold back and just wrote out everything you had to say. Though I also was noticing that both of you were not writing much during the first part of the period today. Instead it seemed like you were sitting and reading a lot. Could you tell me what you were thinking about?"

One of the girls looked back down at her paper and up again, looked at her partner and then looked at me over the dark, thick rims of her glasses. "Well," she began, "I wrote everything that I had to say already."

The other girl's confidence rose with this remark. "Yeah," she added, "I read mine and read it, but I don't really have anything to add. It's already perfect."

The teachers and I had to hold back laughter. On one level they were endearing and such the classic middle schoolers, so committed to their writing that at least one of them was sure it was "perfect"; on the other hand it was clear that they were not yet able to engage with the process of revision. The girls had neither the tools nor the drive to seek out ways to experiment with their work to find what was possible.

You might find students in your own room disengaging because they have not yet internalized the writing process and the habits of mind that go along with it (see Figure 1.1). For some students, it might be that on days for collecting ideas they begin to drift, or perhaps they work on one story idea for so long that they nearly complete a "draft" on the very first day. Or for others, when it is time to revise they stare quietly at their page, not creating a bother, but doing little writing.

Ways of Adjusting Your Teaching

Make Their Efforts Measurable: Create Quantitative Goals

If your writers disengage along points of the writing process, perhaps not getting started or not making the most of their time, consider making their efforts measurable to them. For these writers, try starting them off with quantitative goals rather than purely qualitative ones. As William Zinsser describes in the classic book, *On Writing Well*, "You learn to write by writing. It's a truism, but what makes it a truism is that it's true. The only way to learn to write is to force yourself to produce a certain number of words on a regular basis." If our disengaged writers are sitting staring at blank pages, their writing will never improve. Additionally, it will be hard for you to make teaching decisions from very little writing.

You can provide your writers with opportunities to set measureable goals in a few different ways. One way is to help them visually see how much they have written across a given

	Writing Habits of Mind	In a Narrative Unit of Study (Personal, Genre Fiction, etc.)	In an Essay Unit of Study (Personal, Literary, etc.)
Collecting	Gather way more ideas than you will actually use, so later you can find the ones with the most potential. Allow one idea to lead you to the next.	Gather lots of stories, plots, or characters rather than starting with one story idea and writing out the whole piece.	Gather lots of ideas and write a lot about each one rather than starting with a thesis statement set.
Rehearsing	Try out your ideas, narrowing them down to one. Imagine possible structures, possible starts and ends, and possible details to include.	Try various options for developing characters, then planning out how the story will go. Give each option several attempts before committing to one.	Try various ways of saying the thesis and supports you might use to prove it. Develop a tool to help you gather possible examples.
Drafting	Use all you have discovered and tried out to write one full draft quickly.	Organize or rewrite all of the parts in a possible order. Get all of the words down quickly, knowing you will come back to revise later.	Organize or rewrite all of the parts in a possible order. Get all of the words down quickly, knowing you will come back to revise later.
Revising	Make large, brave changes, not just "fixing what is wrong." Rework the structure, details, and so on to better connect your audience with your central meaning.	Start with meaning and go back to align all parts with that: using strategies such as storytelling the parts that matter more, summarizing other parts, slowing down action at moments of tension, and so forth.	Start with meaning and go back to align all parts of your essay with that: using strategies such as angling examples, reordering paragraphs, composing strong leads and endings, and so on.
Editing	Make sure the words on the page match what you are trying to say so your reader understands your meaning.	Edit for clarity, including checking paragraphs, and so on.	Edit for clarity, including checking paragraphs, and so on.
Publishing/ Celebrating	Allow your writing to be seen by others, to feel that your life and ideas are valuable and worth sharing.	Put your story out for others to read and comment on; collect stories together as a class book and put it in the public library; read it to a sibling.	Type an essay and mail it to someone who should read it; post it in a public place.

FIG. 1.1 *Supporting Our Students' Independence Means Helping Them Develop Writing Habits of Mind in Every Unit of Study*

period of time. For example I might say to a class or to an individual: "Can you point to the last word you wrote on your page? Now, run your finger over to the red line at the margin. Can you place a dot there? Good. Now, can you look down the page and set a goal for yourself of how far you think you can write in five minutes and place an X in that margin? See, look at my notebook. I have a dot here and an X down here because I think I can write half a page or more in the next five minutes. OK, ready? I'll let you know when five minutes has passed."

Like with anything, you will probably want to push some of your more cautious students a little: "Sara, I know you can write farther than that. Why not put the X down here?"

I then make it a point to wait a little longer than five minutes (but still claim the time has been short!). I want my students, especially my disengaged ones, to feel a sense of success from this first goal-setting experience. After eight minutes or so, I gather the entire class and *lie* about the time a little: "OK, stop for a moment. That has been five minutes. How many of you reached your goal?" Usually hands go up, I catch some smiles, and then I put them back to work: "Set a new goal. Let's go for five more minutes. Now remember, you don't have to wait on me to set goals like this. I think many of you found this exercise really helpful. If you ever find yourself feeling like you are losing steam, you can always set a goal in your own mind or on your paper and keep an eye on the time."

You might plan to follow up in writing conferences with a few students, helping them more consistently set these kinds of goals on their own. Additionally, having partners compare goals and how they met them is always an effective motivational tool with middle schoolers. Ultimately, you are helping your students find strategies that they can use again and again, beyond just today's class period.

Another example of setting quantitative goals is to help students plan a number of different ideas. For instance, during the collecting stage of the writing process, you want your writers to collect many, many story ideas—short blips of thinking, several sentences long—but then move on to the next and the next. This way they will not get stuck on just one idea and then "be done" with their entire draft—or worse: commit to a story idea that in the end does not really lead them to much better writing (like the endless summer amusement park trips we all have to read through at the start of each school year). For these writers, I often end a collecting lesson by having them set a quantitative goal: "So writers, today you are going to collect many story ideas, not just one. Set a goal for yourself: decide how many story ideas you think you can collect during this period. I know that most students your age can usually collect something like six, seven, or eight. Would you write on the top of your page the word goal and next to it the number of entries you hope to collect?"

Of course you need to walk around a bit and nudge some who need nudging: "Really, Jessica, only two? I know you can collect more than that. Add a few more to that goal."

This number then becomes a helpful visual and measurable reminder for both the student and for you. I often glance at the goals as I walk around the room or ask about them during conferences. Sometimes I ask students to look back over several days of goals, to help them see if there are patterns emerging or if they are growing beyond their initial abilities. Any chance to compliment is an important one.

You might also suggest that partners reflect together on their goals at the end of the period: "Writers, can you look at your writing from today and ask yourself, Did I meet my goal today? Then, can you think about what you did during this period and in your notebook that either helped you meet it or got in the way? I would like you to talk with your partner about what you are noticing about yourself, and then I would like you to talk about what you could do differently tomorrow. Then jot one thing you will try tomorrow on the top of a new notebook page."

I have actually learned a lot of new strategies from students doing this. For example, students in a school in Chicago taught me that when jotting down story ideas during collecting, they should start with the most important parts, instead of starting from the very beginning of the memory, so they do not have to write out so much for each idea.

To support your students in making their efforts measurable and visible for them, you can:

- ▶ Have them create goals for the amount of writing they will try to do in a short amount of time
- ▶ Suggest they create goals for the number of ideas they will try, like the number of different ideas they will collect and write about
- ▶ Have them reflect with you and with partners on their goals and what they have done to try to meet them

Reframe Revision: Make It an Act of Experimentation, Not Correction

A strange thing sometimes happens when it comes time to revise: our students morph from being creative, eccentric, vibrant human beings into dull, thoughtless photocopiers. Oftentimes even our strongest writers place their "rough draft" to their left, a clean sheet of paper to their right, and then go line by line, rewriting verbatim what they had written before—only "fixing" a few things here and there. Maybe adding a bunch of adjectives to the kind of jacket their friend was wearing: *"a large, blue and white, Yankees jacket."* Or adding in a small bit of dialogue as you had taught them in the day's lesson: *My mom was angry with me* turns into *"I am so angry with you," my mom said.*

It is clear that there are some troubles with this behavior: their writing is clearly not getting much better, even if that is what they set out to do. Second, an enormous amount of class time is being wasted just copying what they had already written—an in-class version of mindless television rerun watching. There is no progress for the writer or the writing. Last, disengagement runs high, resulting in the often repeated, "but my writing is fine; I already changed everything that needed to be changed."

Luckily, by adjusting your instruction, you can help your students become better at revising. Everything revolves around an overhaul of how you think about revision in your classroom. Instead of having your students make multiple drafts, consider having them create just one that contains all the revisions. Instead of making revision about *correcting errors*, talk about revision as *running experiments*, more experiments than they will ever actually use in the end.

One break-through moment in my own teaching came from studying with the Teachers College Reading and Writing Project and learning ways to have my students stop making so many drafts. In the beginning I didn't know any better; it was what I had done when I was a student. The teacher would assign "draft one" to be due on a Wednesday, "draft two" on the following Tuesday, "draft three" on Friday, and the "final draft" due the next week after that. At first, I did the same kind of assignments for my students. However, a few issues resulted, all of which I realized were the same reactions I had when I was in school. As a classroom teacher, I would hand back each draft, pages marked up with my corrections. Then, a good percentage of my students would become photocopiers for an entire class period (or sometimes more if they were really trying to avoid writing) and simply make the adjustments that I had already thought through for them. A few days later, they would turn in that new "draft" for another go. Of course, this meant they did not learn much about looking at their own writing. What the Reading and Writing Project taught me to do instead was to have them use only one main draft that all of the revisions would be added to.

To set up this draft so it supports your students' future revisions, ask them to write on only one side of each page of draft paper. It also helps if they skip every other line, so shorter revisions can be added in between lines. Then, when they go to revise, you can teach them to write between the lines, perhaps on the back of the page, or—most important—on small strips of draft paper (something like a fourth to a half of a page of regular lined paper). These strips can be stapled or taped right to the draft. I find it helpful to have students code these strips and to write the codes inside the body of their draft—like adding a star or a number "1" to the first strip they experimented with, then label the same place in the draft so they can be matched up later. What all of this means is that students now have the entire class time to work on writing without the wasted copying time.

Next, anywhere you go across the country, when it comes to middle schoolers it is all about how you say things; a terrific teacher I work with in a school in New York City calls it "having a great sales pitch." Saying, "now I want you to revise" often translates to our disengaged writers as, "you have fought tooth and nail to try and avoid writing every day, but I forced you through it anyway; after so much agony you completed a draft that you don't love but you don't really hate either, it is now time for you to go back and figure out all the things that are totally wrong with it and change everything." I think subtly, or sometimes not so subtly, we suggest that revision is about correcting: adding in dialogue because it "is missing"; changing the description of any action because it "is unclear"; making a stronger lead because it "isn't a grabber." Also, our minilessons and conferences often contain only these small changes because we are trying to keep them short. For our students to engage with revision we need to make it something bigger and more purposeful.

Talking with Your Students

When beginning a process of revision, I often talk to classes in this way:

(You might engage them first with a new way of thinking about revision and then teach them one tool to support this. You might find it helpful to play up their "being older and wiser" as a way to distinguish between how they thought about revision in the past and how they will think about it now.)

"Today we are going to begin the process of revision. In previous years, you may have thought about revision as changing little things to make your writing 'better.' Your teacher might have asked you to find places that did not have any examples of what the characters were thinking and so you went and changed those places. This year, though, now that you are becoming young adults and ready to think about writing in a whole new way, I want to suggest to you a new way of revising in which we won't just 'fix stuff.' Instead we will do what writers in the world do: we will run experiments with our writing. We will try out one big change, then a totally different one, then another different other one, to see what new idea we have."

(Sometimes it is helpful to give a life example for an abstract concept to make it feel more concrete.)

"Think about when you go shopping for clothes for the start of school. You stand in front of the dressing room mirror, with a pile of shirts and pants or shorts or dresses. You think to yourself, 'Who do I want to be this year? What kind of me do I want to show other people?' You maybe try on a shirt you know your mom will approve of because it's like the ones you usually wear. Then you try on a different one that you picked up that has a huge lion across the shoulder and rips on the arms—it looks so tough, but you wonder if it's over the top. You then think, maybe you will try something without the rips, but you like the big graphic—you don't normally wear things like that. And so on it goes. Each outfit you try on is an experiment; you learn from some, you put back others, but each one is helping you learn more about yourself and how you want to be seen. This is the same way we are going to approach revision this year, just like standing in that dressing room on August 29th, experimenting with our new look."

(Describe a tool your students can use to support this kind of experimentation, then model how you would use it in your own writing.)

"One way we are going to experiment is by using small sheets of paper. Instead of just picking up one and saying, 'I am now going to add dialogue, write, write, write, OK done,' we are going to pick up a few at a time and treat each as a new experiment. Let me show you how I can do this with my own piece. Let's use a strategy we already know from the last unit of study. This time, however, I am going to try out several versions, a bunch of experiments all in one place of my draft. OK, so first . . ."

Creating an image of revision that is more about experimenting freely and less about correcting helps our writers take more risks than they may have otherwise. The feeling of "experiment" suggests that you are just trying out a few things to see what happens, but you are not bound to anything. To support this, in your conferences you will probably want to coach students to try more than one experiment in any given place. For example, when I see them finish one experiment, I quickly grab a second sheet of paper and say, "OK, now what are you going to do for a second experiment? How are you going to write that same section again, only differently?" From here you can imagine a litany of strategies, like rewriting the same scene showing the character's emotions through inner thinking, then trying another where it is symbolized through setting; changing the character's motivation in the scene to see how it plays out differently; making a secondary character more prominent or even varying who is in a particular scene.

To reframe the revision process in your room, invite students to:

- Use only one draft that all revisions are written in, on, and attached to
- Draft in a way that allows them to more easily add in revisions later, such as skipping lines and writing on only one side of the page
- Think of revisions as experiments, running several in the same place in different ways, possibly using multiple strips of paper

Connect Them with Texts They Love: Help Them Apprentice Themselves to Books They Admire

For any of us, being able to visualize the end result makes the journey to it so much more purposeful and motivating. Seeing master chef Jacques Pépin lift the cover off a beautiful bouillabaisse makes you want to commit to chopping all of the ingredients. Seeing that outfit on the mannequin inspires you to try it on. Meeting with a friend who has recently lost weight helps you see yourself going to the gym a bit more. Having a full vision of where you are headed helps all of us engage with the tasks leading up to it.

For our disengaged writers it is no different. If you can provide them with opportunities—especially engaging ones—to see where they will end up, you are helping them to take on the harder parts. While teaching using "mentor texts" is commonplace in many vibrant writing classrooms (Ray 1999), I know many of us often think of these as texts *we choose* for students to use. For our middle school writers these teacher-chosen books are always helpful, but they can still appear as "being in the writers' club," a club in which our disengaged writers often do not place themselves. Consider not only using texts you select but tapping into the power of the books and magazines students have whole-heartedly selected for themselves.

We are lucky that young adult reading has been having such a resurgence in recent years. The number of engaging novels with appealing topics continues to grow. Worldwide book phenomena like *Harry Potter* and *Twilight* are a prime part of our students' social lives. Look no further than the aisles of your nearest bookstore or, if you are lucky, the young adult section of your public library if they happen to have a good one, and you will most likely see teens sitting around reading, asking for authors by name, running to get the next title of a hot series. Their engagement with text is high, so connecting it to their own writing lives is a natural fit.

Sure, if we develop our own demonstration writing to be more varied, more personal, and more engaging we will grab many more of our writers (see Chapter 2 for more on this). But sometimes, for our most disengaged students, our writing is not enough at first. Helping our students look at their current, best-loved reading (or if they are not as in love with books as we would hope them to be, we can pull from what is "hot" and "now" among their peers) as examples to apprentice themselves to has major traction in our writing workshop. If Stephenie Meyer writes like that, maybe I can, too.

One first, simple step to take in making this method a larger part of your practice is to hold conferences during the editing process. If a student is having trouble, say, punctuating dialogue, you could repeat to them the same rules that they have probably been hearing for years *or* you could simply grab a book. I often have a quick conference in this way. Once I know the issue—such as dialogue punctuation, as in this case—I usually ask the student to grab the book they are reading now. I will say something like:

Talking with Your Students

(Set up the writer to have an inquiry with you by laying out the focus and giving some tips on what to look for.)

"Can you turn to where you are in your book now? I want to see if we can find a section that you have read recently that has a bunch of dialogue in it. When we find it, can we look together to see how this author punctuates what someone says and lets us know who is saying it? Let's look together at the marks that are used, the order the parts are in, what is capitalized, and anything else you notice."

[Student looks and finds a place.]

"OK, you found a spot. This will help us a lot because there are a few characters speaking here. Let's look together. What do you notice?"

(After naming the parts, leave the book open and invite the writer to try punctuating his or her piece in the same way. Make

the most of this connection to a book the student is reading by talking up how she is like the author. Be sure to stay with the student a bit, while she tries it out.)

"You noticed that Jacqueline Woodson in the book *Hush* uses quotes around what is being said, and sometimes there is a comma, sometimes a period, sometimes a question mark. And you noticed that sometimes she writes the name of who is speaking and sometimes she stops that after a while. Can you do something for me? Can you keep your book open to this page and go back to your draft. Let's see if you can write your dialogue in the same way Jacqueline Woodson does in this book. Before you start, tell me what you are going to try . . ."

It is a great motivation for many of our students to imagine themselves writing like the authors they love, and the book becomes a constant model for them, meaning you do not have to always be by their side. You could take this same idea and expand it beyond just looking for punctuation. In a conference with a strong seventh-grade writer in a school I consult with in Queens, New York, the teacher and I were having trouble thinking of what to teach next. The class was in the revision process during a Fantasy writing unit and the student's piece was clearly one of the most well crafted and well devised. We read her description of a girl descending the staircase at a university where things were not always what they seemed, and we looked at each other and mouthed, "Wow!" We, like the writer, thought there was not much more to do. We could have simply decided to leave the conference at that point. Instead we thought to talk with her a bit about the *Twilight* series, which clearly she was emulating.

I told her about a point in her draft that was not as clear to me. "You might have explained it somewhere else, but in the part you read, I am not so sure how I, as the reader, am supposed to feel about those people she sees walking down in the courtyard." The girl explained that she had described it earlier and showed me the part, which simply summarized that they were a "human-demon mix." I then asked her to tell me about what she liked about *Twilight*. Her face lit up.

"Well," she said, "I love how you can feel what Bella is feeling, how her thoughts are really clear, and you feel nervous when she feels nervous. She seems a lot like me, sometimes. I feel like I really know her."

We both knew we had found something important to work on. "Do you think you might be able to do the same thing with your draft?"

"I mean, yeah, I could try to show more of the girl's feelings, what she is thinking. Yeah!" She went to work.

When you pull in books, even nonfiction, that students are already in love with, the potential for what to think about in a conference is endless. You might have students consider the way a book is organized, like the alternating timelines of Angela Johnson's *The First Part Last*; how you learn about characters, like the way a character's actions evolve across the Rick Riordan series, *Percy Jackson and the Olympians*; how ideas are grouped together by sections in a video game magazine; or even how the personality of the writer often comes through in those articles. Adding "talk about books" to your writing conference to-do list can bring your students from a feeling of writing as being only for the classroom to an understanding of how writing touches their lives.

To help students apprentice themselves to books they admire, you might:

▶ Treat the interaction with their book like an inquiry, setting up the lenses to look through and then allowing them to describe what they see

▶ Look to their books for both small, section-specific ideas, as well as larger whole-piece organization

▶ Stay with them for a bit during the conference as they try out what they just discovered, so you can coach them and refer back to the text if they need support

CHAPTER TWO

Writers Who Just Cannot Find Anything to Write About at All

This chapter will help you to:

▶ Be certain to model for everyone: vary your demonstration texts

▶ Help them see their potential: use the power of your own storytelling

▶ Develop student confidence: build ownership in compliment conferences

Case Study

I was in a seventh-grade classroom outside of Charlotte, North Carolina, a few years ago. The teachers were concerned about the unfortunate reality of high-stakes testing; seventh grade, it turned out, was the only grade level to have a writing test in the North Carolina middle schools at that time. Traditionally, they would pour their lives into preparing their students the best way they knew—hours and hours of drills and tricks for different kinds of essays. The teachers were burnt out; the students were burnt out. We spoke for quite some time about the importance of narrative writing as a basis for learning to write anything, as well as the natural progression a school year might take from narrative to essay and back again and again through different genres. They loved the idea—after all, they were an incredible teaching team—but they were also afraid of taking away time from preparation. The pressures of standardized testing loomed larger than life.

In an act of what could be described as pure bravery, the team agreed to try out some narrative writing with their class. During one visit we gathered in a classroom and the teacher pointed out a few students to me informally. "She writes all the time at home. You have to really be on top of him." The last student she pointed to was a young man, busy flirting with the girl two desks over. "He claims he has nothing to write about. He barely writes for test prep, too. It's like pulling teeth."

I sat in front of the class and started the lesson: a simple way of generating writing ideas for narrative writing by thinking about people who matter in your life and moments you have had with them. "So one person in my life was Aimee." I wrote her name on my list and then started to tell about her. "She was the love of my life in high school." The class said the predictable "ooooo"s (and other comments not fit for print). I continued, "One moment I remember with her is when I went over to her house." Again, the middle school sound track continued. "We sat on the couch. But, instead of her looking at me like she normally did, she kept looking away. She wouldn't make eye contact. And finally, after a few quiet minutes, she looked up. Looked me in the eye. And said, 'Chris, We need to talk.'" At this point the class couldn't contain themselves. "Oh, dang. You're in trouble now, mister."

I wrapped up the lesson and the class returned to their seats to write. The teachers and I then stood at the side of the classroom, quietly observing behaviors. We noticed something amazing: our friend who "never has anything to write about" sat down to work and didn't lift his head once. I remember the curriculum coordinator and I saw him first. "Look!" she said to me. "Look at him go!"

Ways of Adjusting Your Teaching

Be Certain to Model for Everyone: Vary Your Demonstration Texts

Sometimes our writers who struggle to find topics to write about just have not seen themselves as writers. In a speech David Booth (2009) gave at a summer writing institute at Teachers College he spoke about how today it is amazing that all of us can find our lives portrayed inside of published books. He said that in the past the kinds of characters and plots were generally very limited and almost alienating to the vast majority of us. Today, however, every one of us at every age can find characters that look like us, act like us, struggle over what we struggle over. He urged the audience to tap into this amazing gift, to help our students see themselves and learn about themselves through books. This point, though intended for reading, cannot be lost on us for writing.

If we model stories that seem foreign and disconnected from our students' lives, then they will not be able to imagine themselves writing their own stories. If we write about too adult topics, like our wedding, they may not be able to see themselves within it. Or if we always write deeply emotional, self-reflective stories, we will be missing those students who connect best to humor or to stories of triumph. My colleague and mentor, Mary Ehrenworth, author of several books including *The Power of Grammar* (with Vinton 2005), has spoken about this often with teachers. She says that we have to write about the kinds of issues that are hidden in our classrooms if we ever want to see them come out.

This process begins by researching ourselves a bit. For example, when I look back over a unit, or even several units of writing workshop, I find that I tend to demonstrate writing topics that reveal some sort of personal weakness or a feeling of having one. I often write about being bullied in seventh grade, about confrontations with my father growing up, about being dumped by a girlfriend. I write about these topics because I believe that they are general themes most of my students can connect with. Though at the same time, when really reflecting on my teaching, I realize that they are sort of one note. True, many middle school students *are* moody and are going through a period a deep self-reflection, but that does not mean that every student wants to write about moments of self-loathing. If you find students in your room are having trouble finding topics, look carefully at the kinds of topics you demonstrate and then, as I learned from Mary, be strategic in the ways you adjust them.

If you notice that many of your topics are about your adult life—marriage, kids, having a job, buying a home—you might include demonstration texts that are more focused on what your desires and concerns were as a middle schooler. This could go one of two ways. One, you might just include stories from your life when you were a student, such as incidents in class, arguments with your parents, or changing friendships. Two, you could take the emotional story from that adult moment and repackage it from a student perspective. For example, an argument with your spouse could be repackaged as an argument with your parent about extending your curfew. Or the feelings of butterflies and excitement on your wedding day could be rewritten as the feelings you might have had during your first big school dance in sixth grade. This is not to say that in personal narrative writing, you would completely make things up. Chances are the feelings you feel in the argument with your partner have some similarities to the feelings you felt in other arguments with people who really mattered across your life.

If you notice that your stories do mirror the age level of your students, you might then look at the kinds of emotional tones you tend to write about and vary those. For example, if you are like me and tend to write about emotionally tortured middle school experiences, then you might consider having a larger range of emotions, including some stories that are just plain funny, some that are about a moment of triumph and celebration, and some that are of discovery and personal understanding.

To help students find topics to write about, they need to see themselves in our lessons. They need to be able to imagine themselves doing what we are doing, collecting stories that matter to them, drafting and revising them.

When varying your demonstration pieces keep your students' interests in mind:

- Ask yourself if your demonstration pieces are ones your students could see themselves in
- Bring emotional moments from your adult life, but repackage them as student experiences you had
- Look for patterns in your demonstration pieces; if you have fallen into a rut of repeated topics or emotional moods, vary them

Help Them See Their Potential: Use the Power of Your Own Storytelling

When working to help our writers find their own stories, we want to help them to not only see topics but also imagine how their own writing might go. We need to make sure that the writing we demonstrate, whether it be narratives or essay ideas or snippets of poems, grabs their attention and helps them see what is possible.

As with anything, base your decisions on what you are noticing about your writers. For example, if I notice my disengaged writers have trouble getting started, even after I showed a good example of my own writing, then I might decide to create more of my piece in front of my students instead of just putting up a completely written entry on the overhead or flipping to a finished piece written on chart paper. When you put up a completely written entry it sort of looks like magic at best, or like way too much to accomplish at worst. Our disengaged writers already are having trouble seeing themselves *as writers*, so putting up a huge amount of well-crafted writing can add to their anxiety.

Also true, however, is that I try to not write too much in front of them. I am guilty of becoming so invested in my own writing that I scribble, scribble, scribble on a piece of chart paper and then turn a few minutes later to find half my class has zoned way out. Instead, I often write a bit and then raise my pen and keep telling the story.

Last, whether you are just jumping into demonstrating more of your writing in front of your students or if you have been teaching using workshop methods for years, one of the suggestions I give most to teachers is to tell your story for just a little bit longer than you think you should. My gauge, usually, is that I keep telling my story or idea until I start to see physical signs of engagement from my most disengaged students: sitting up a little, laughing, blurting out. When that happens, I think "got 'em!" and get ready to transition into the next part of my lesson. This method runs parallel to how you are teaching them to craft their stories or flesh out their essay ideas, to tell detail by engaging detail—the tried and true "show not tell" method—to help your reader invest in the experience. I want my demonstration writing to hold the same tension, carry the same emotional arch, and dive into the same detail as I want for their drafts.

In addition to carefully crafting how I tell the story, I also want to tell the story of my thinking. Again, I advise you to say more than you might think is enough. The pauses and "hmms" and pondering a bit, when authentically matching how you actually hear your own voice in your head, demonstrates for students the process of a writer, inviting them to develop the same kinds of thinking in their minds. Oftentimes for our most disengaged writers there is a feeling that when the pen hits the page the words should somehow just flow freely—when they don't, road blocks are set up. Showing your writers how you process your ideas helps them to do this for themselves (see more about this in Chapter 4).

Talking with Your Students

Here is one example of how a lesson might go in this way:

(You might already have a list jotted on chart paper. It could have a "People" column and a "Moments" column and a few things written underneath each. Be certain to remind your students that you do not just make lists all day long but that you get to writing as quickly as possible.)

"OK, now I have my list. But I don't want to stop there. On any writing day my job is to jot fast so I can get straight to longer writing. Some days I may not jot a list of ideas at all; I might jump right into writing. So let me try this out fast. I'm going to draw a line underneath my lists from yesterday. Then I'll circle one and start writing. Hmmm . . . let's see. Which one could I say a lot about right now? Well, I could start with the one about Aimee."

(Show them how writers do not just drop their pens to the page

and hope for the best. Instead they might quickly decide a way or place to start and replay that moment a little in their minds. Think through this out loud so they can see your process.)

"OK, so how could I start? Hmmm . . . where were we? We were in her house. I came to the door and she was there, but she didn't really look at me that much. We walked over to her family room; it was kind of dark there. There was a green couch, I think I remember, or maybe it was black. We'd usually watch TV there. So, I remember I walked in and sat down, but she was kind of standing for a little bit, right by the hallway leading in. So maybe I write something like, 'There I was, sitting . . .' OK, let me start writing with that."

(Next show them how your entry starts. For our disengaged writers—though, frankly, for any of us—this can be the toughest spot. So, choose to write this part out in front of them. Write the next small bit quickly and then stop writing, but keep telling, and turn your body to the class.)

"There I was, sitting on the big black couch. Aimee stood in the hallway; she didn't come over at first. *What was I thinking at that moment? Oh yeah . . .* I thought to myself, 'Wow, she looks so good, standing there in the light. I'm so lucky.' But she stood there for a moment. This was so strange. I looked up at her, hoping she'd smile back, like she always did."

(At a moment like this, stop writing, but continue to tell the story. Turn to the class and as you story-tell, look for signs of engagement. Make eye contact to draw students in. Use your body to show your actions, what your face looked like, where you were looking. Modulate your voice, pace, volume, and pitch to show your emotions. You want this short moment to be as captivating as possible.)

"Finally, she turned slightly and looked at me. Her eyes seemed strange: they kept looking away and then back again. My heart started racing. I kept looking at her. 'Aimee, are you

OK?' I asked. She cleared her throat. She spoke, 'Chris,' she started. 'Chris, um . . . we need to talk.'"

I tried to accomplish a few things through this demonstration. I wanted to make sure that I was using a story that students could find a connection with. I wanted to show them that writers write like they are there, in the moment, not just summarizing it. I wanted to engage my writers, especially those who feel that they often have nothing to write about. And I wanted them to start imagining themselves writing their own stories. I tried to find a moment they could connect with, one full of tension and energy. I highlighted those feelings by both writing in front of them and by using my voice and body. Stretching these moments out, lingering a bit in the process of thinking, usually leads to pencils almost uncontrollably scratching across notebook pages. You are showing your students what is possible; oftentimes as you tell your story they are playing out their own in their heads.

When using your own storytelling to help students see the power of writing you might:

- ❱ Do some writing in front of your students, instead of putting up your completed pieces, so they see your process
- ❱ Keep them engaged and bring energy to your story by stopping at some point in your writing, but continue telling your story out loud
- ❱ Use everything you know about good writing as you tell your story aloud, using your voice and body to help them feel lost in your moment or idea

Develop Student Confidence: Build Ownership in Compliment Conferences

I am sure you know the essential, sometimes even life-changing, role you play for your students. After all, it is a reason so many of us chose to teach, and, in particular, to teach at the middle school level. We remember what life was like for us during this time and we choose to teach our students to make their experiences better than our own. Sometimes when our writers say they have nothing to write about, or if they instead just use less productive coping strategies, I often believe that it represents a lack of confidence in their writing more than anything else.

Whenever I am faced with students who feel disengaged with writing and believe they have nothing at all to write about, I turn to the power of conferences, the time you make during your class period to have individual conversations with writers—what I consider to be the engine that drives your teaching (Graves 1983; Calkins 1994; Anderson 2000). One type of conference that is particularly powerful for lifting up our most disengaged writers is the "compliment conference." They tend to be shorter than most conferences, so you can easily add them into your regular classroom routine. The compliment conference has three main steps: research what the writers are doing, decide on one thing that they are doing really well, then describe what they are doing to help them see it and continue to use it.

In *Choice Words*, Peter H. Johnston (2004) describes this kind of careful teacher observation as noticing the "leading edge" of the student's work, finding a point "where the student has reached beyond herself, stretching what she knows just beyond its limit, producing something that is partly correct." He goes on to add, "This is the launching pad for new learning." It is an opportunity to give confidence to a writer who may not often feel it, as well as teaching her a strategy in a stealthy fashion.

You might sit next to one of your disengaged writers and ask what he is working on or read a little bit over his shoulder. As you talk and read, ask yourself, "What is something this writer is doing that he may not even realize he is doing but is making him stronger than he was before?" Once you've found that something, you might interrupt the writer and tell him what you noticed, describing it clearly. When I describe what he is doing, I have a rule of thumb: point to it, describe it, and keep talking until the writer smiles.

To some teachers, this prospect at first feels a bit hokey in description. "You mean I'm just going to go around and say how nice everything is?" they sometimes ask. The point is not just to be caring—though that is still part of it. The point is to highlight something you want your students to continue to do. Take, for example, if someone compliments something you are wearing. A colleague of mine once said to me, "That shirt looks really nice on you. Blue is a great color on you." Of course, naturally, I now own quite a few blue shirts. Every time I open my closet and am looking for something to wear I actually think, "Well, I know I look good in blue." Whether she realized it, she taught me a strategy for fashion that I continue to use. This goes for writing as well.

One of my former students, who I will call Candice, had a really rough go in life. Her living arrangements changed many times over only a few years. Not only was she barely engaged in writing, she was barely engaged in class, in teachers, in school. She exhibited poor writing skills and would quickly try to avoid anything that made her feel like a failure. I was not sure if we would make much progress together that year, but I considered starting with simple, short compliment conferences as the initial way to go. I vividly remember one of the first ones I had with her; it went something like this:

Talking with Your Students

(Interrupt the writer and ask her to talk to you about her work. As you listen and read over her shoulder, think about one thing the writer is doing that feels new and important to her growth. This is not time to think of her in comparison to every other writer in your room, but instead to think about her in comparison only to herself. Where was she before and where is she now in this moment?)

"Candice, can I interrupt you for a minute? Could you just tell me a bit about what you are working on? I know you are revising your personal narrative. Could you tell me what you are trying to do?"

"Um. Uh. I don't know. I'm just kind of writing."

"Mm-hmm. I see, can you show me where, what sorts of things you are writing?"

"Right here. I was just, like, writing about my uncle or something."

(For our more disengaged writers, verbalizing what they are doing can be difficult. You may need to rely more on what you see in their writing, at first, and then transition them into more conversation about their process as the year goes on. Once you find something to compliment, try to point to it, describe it, and keep talking until the writer literally smiles.)

"Hold on a minute, can I read this part back to you? This part right here, where your uncle is talking. Here, listen.

[I read a small bit of dialogue, reading it to show how I really, really enjoy it.] 'Hey,' he said, 'What's all that racket out there?' Wow, Candice, let me read that again. 'Hey,' he said, 'What's all that racket out there?' Did you notice what I noticed?"

"What?"

"The way you write dialogue reminds me a lot of how Walter Dean Myers writes dialogue. He writes trying to capture exactly what people sound like. A lot of writers try to do that, but it is really hard to do. Some even take special courses or get coaching from other writers on how to make characters sound like real people. But just like Walter Dean Myers, the way you write dialogue, like at this point, makes it sound just like your uncle would actually talk. It doesn't sound fake to me. It sounds like I can actually hear him, I can picture him. The way you write dialogue, trying to carefully make it sound just like the real person, is something most writers dream of doing. I am so proud of you."

It may sound like a lot, even a bit unnatural, but this is just the way I try to speak to disengaged writers, even those who seem to be the least interested in writing. If you notice, I did not then move on to teach anything else. I did not say, "Now I want you to notice that when you punctuate dialogue you can't forget to use quotation marks." Half the battle for our most disengaged writers is just writing, and sometimes our well-purposed teaching suggestions can be received as, "Remember everything I just said? I didn't mean any of it. Here's the problem with your writing." Candice left that conference with a smile and then started writing more than she had on most days. For Candice, I held several compliment conferences across several weeks. Her overall engagement with writing, with me, with the class, began to transform.

In this conference I compared her to an author I knew she admired. I also read her writing out loud to her, savoring the lines. I also could have responded as her reader, letting her know how her writing affected me, "As a reader, I really feel like I know your uncle because the words you have him say sound like a real person, like someone I know even." Or instead I could have spoken about choices she did not make as a way to highlight the ones she did: "What I just love is that you could have just written something like 'my uncle was mad,' but instead you had him speak. And you didn't just have him say anything; you allowed him to use the words you know he uses." In all of these instances being specific and supportive, pointing, describing, and saying enough words to make the writer smile pays huge dividends for that writer and for your classroom.

To build student ownership using compliment conferences, remember:

- ▶ Ask questions to find out what the writer is working on or read over her shoulder
- ▶ Ask yourself, "What is this writer almost doing or just beginning to do that is new and powerful?"
- ▶ Be specific in your compliment: point to the part you are talking about, describe exactly what the writer is doing, and keep talking until he smiles

CHAPTER THREE

Writers Who Talk, Talk, Talk the Writing Time Away

This chapter will help you to:

- ▶ Clearly divide talk time and writing time: set a "partner time" routine
- ▶ Angle and support the conversations they do have: teach strategically into partner talk
- ▶ Value their need for immediate conversations: create a partner spot

Case Study

During one period in an eighth-grade classroom in New York, a cadre of teachers and I stood at the front of the room, shortly after the minilesson, and watched as the class slowly morphed from silently and busily writing in their notebooks, to a few brief turns of the head to one another, to a sudden eruption of chatter from all corners.

"Look at them, they're at it again! Every day they all just want to start talking right in the middle of everything," the classroom teacher said with obvious exhaustion.

I turned to the group and set the plan, "OK. Let's take a minute and just walk around, listen to what they are talking about, notice who they are talking to and how often, and let's come back together and share what we found. We will probably find a lot in a short amount of time. And then together we can try to figure out what's at the bottom of all this." We walked around the room and a few moments later came back.

One teacher started, "Well, when I walked over there, Xavier was in the middle of telling some of the stories from his collecting list to Josh. The trouble was he didn't have much writing on his page."

"I guess I noticed kind of the same thing," another teacher added. "Sara told a little bit about the story idea she was jotting and kept asking her neighbors if it sounded good."

I was surprised. I assumed they were chatting about everything *except* writing. It turned out, many (sure not all, but many) were actually talking *about* writing. We had discovered something important. I said to the teachers: "So in this instance, it is true that they are really talkative. But the funny thing is that their conversations seem to be really valuable. They aren't just talking about what they did this weekend or gossiping about friends. Instead, most of them are actually talking about their writing, even asking each other about it. They feel safe to share with one another and ask questions, they seem to really desire the ability to talk with one another.

The trouble is that while they are talking, no one is really getting much of anything written. So, probably what we should think about are some structures to put in place in the room that allow them to talk with one another and help each other with their writing—because they value it and actually are pretty good at it—but, we should also find ways to make a clear separation between talk time and writing time so they get words written on the page."

What follows are some ways to support your students' desire for conversation, while angling this talk to help them grow as writers.

Ways of Adjusting Your Teaching

Clearly Divide Talk Time and Writing Time: Set a "Partner Time" Routine

One solution we immediately created during that chatty class period was to acknowledge the students' desire to communicate about their writing while also providing a quiet, focused space to accomplish that writing. We instituted daily time for students to talk with one another during writing workshop, a structure that teachers who work with the Reading and Writing Project have come to know well, though often find challenging to keep to. This conversation time is not just a great management technique for your classroom, it is an essential skill of writing, what Peter Elbow describes as "cooking" ideas between two people so that the writer can end up "seeing, feeling, and knowing things he hadn't thought of before" (1998).

This time to converse could happen at any point, but it might feel like a good end to the class period. For instance, you may commit to reserve around five minutes of class time at the end of *every* writing period for students to talk together about their work. If you make this a daily routine, then your students will come to expect that they will have time to talk with one another. For younger students, partner time often translates to simple conversations between peers; with older students, however, there is an added bonus: you and I both know, it is much easier for our middle school writers to ignore us than it is for them to ignore each other! Knowing they will share their writing with a peer usually leads to a visible boost in productivity during the writing period. For instance, in one classroom in New Jersey a young man turned to his writing partner and tried to speed through a sloppy explanation of his essay work for the day. She interrupted him and said, "You and I both know you didn't do much of anything today. What are you going to do tomorrow?" The lesson had been learned!

Your first and most essential task is to actually make time for this practice daily. Unfortunately, in many classrooms it is the first routine to be eliminated as the period flies by and suddenly the bell rings. To keep this time carefully reserved, think of this structure not as a simple add-on to the period but as its own special curriculum across your year—a curriculum to help students communicate better about their writing. Think about how much of our adult lives is consumed by oral communication. Meetings, phone conversations, workshops—our lives require us to be active listeners and careful speakers. Adding this talk time into your class period not only is a way to support writing, it is a way to support a necessary life skill. Give working on better conversation its due.

First decide what consistent, expected time of day to hold this routine. For some classrooms this may be the form that your usual end-of-period "writing share" will take; for other classrooms a few extra minutes can be added before or after that share time (Calkins 1994). For still others, you might prefer to have a time for partners at some other point in your period—like before the minilesson—or even at a different point in your day—like during homeroom at the start of the school day. Regardless of when you decide to place this essential time, keep it consistent and expected. Perhaps add it into your daily lesson plan template or write it on a publically posted agenda. Having the agenda public means you can simply point to the spot on the agenda that says "partner talk time" without even having to say, "You will have time to talk today, just not right now."

If you are anything like me, you find yourself juggling so much during a class period, or so engrossed in writing conferences, that you may occasionally lose track of time. If this is the case, assign a dependable student monitor to let you know when partner time is approaching.

To keep the "Partner Time" routine so your students
come to expect and prepare for it:

▶ Think of this time as its own, essential curriculum that will grow across the year

- Add "Partner Time" to your daily lesson plan template and perhaps even post it as part of a public agenda in the room
- Choose a student monitor to signal you when the time is approaching

Angle and Support the Conversations They Do Have: Teach Strategically into Partner Talk

Making this time a consistent part of your writing period may, in itself, be enough to reengage many of your writers. They know that they have a regular opportunity to share their writing with someone else, and they know when that time is scheduled so they can plan to have some work done to share. You can simply place this time on auto-pilot, and each day let students talk as they will. We can help interactions go better and help partners grow effectively together with a few careful adjustments to our teaching.

You might, for instance, continue to think about these conversations as a curriculum that grows across the year. This curriculum will most likely be built around the writing process, helping your writers consider ways of thinking together about their writing as they move from collecting ideas, to rehearsing some, to committing to an idea and drafting it, to revising and editing their draft, to ultimately publishing and celebrating. In her book on reading workshop in middle school, *Shades of Meaning*, Donna Santman (2005) writes about how she carefully plans her teaching around conversations, including studying her students and having them study each other while they talk. She finds these conversations essential to her teaching because they support not only stronger reading but also student engagement. She writes, "Kids are so easily influenced by each other. They tend to wear the same clothing, and listen to the same music. . . . I knew I could bank on this group power." To develop this practice in your classroom, you could study yourself as you work on stages of the writing process and decide what your partners could say and do to help each other have similar experiences.

For example, because "collecting" is an opportunity to try out many different possible story ideas, consider ways your partners can act as a sounding board for one another, helping to find ideas that hold the most writing potential. You could begin a chart that you post in your room and add to across days, even across the year, to suggest ways that partners can work together during collecting.

You want to help your partners have the most successful interactions as possible. For instance, teach them to turn their notebooks so partners can look at the words they are reading out loud. Show your partners ways of being with each other, almost like roles to play, which they can choose from the chart as more are added each day. For example, I establish a handful of roles early in the year that help to bring partners closer together: complimenting, encouraging, and asking. Let them know that each day, once one partner is done, if there is time, they can switch; otherwise, the writer who did not share can go first the next day. When I am starting out with a class, there are a few things I usually say:

Talking with Your Students

(Let your students know you are establishing a time and a routine for Partner Time within the class—a routine that they can expect will last the year.)

"Now we are going to end our writing workshop the way we will end most writing workshops: meeting with your partner to share what you have been working on. Today, you have an important role to play, so listen carefully. First, when you turn to share, make sure you turn your notebook so your partner can easily see your writing, just like this *(model turning your own notebook to face the class)*. Then, if you are going to read your writing, be careful to read exactly what is on the page—not just talk about it."

(Teach your partnerships a way to interact. Add this way to a "Ways Partners Talk During Collecting" chart you hang up every time your students return to this stage of the writing process. As you talk, tuck in suggestions for how often and in what ways your partners can share their comments.)

"Finally—and here is the really important part—today while you are the listener you have an essential role. Your job is to listen for all of the parts of the writing that you find really engaging. Listen and read along carefully, searching for parts you really enjoy. From what I saw today, I'm sure you will find at least two, though probably more. Then, your job is to stop the writer every time you get to one of those points: just go ahead and interrupt him, and say, 'Stop right there! I love that part! mark it!' Writers, when your partner stops you at a part she enjoys, stop and be sure to underline it or star it or mark it however you'd like. OK? Let's go."

At this point every day, your role is to make your way around the room, listening into partnerships. Some will have the knack of this really quickly and you will just give a silent thumbs up or a nod. Others, you will notice, just stay frozen, one partner reading while the other is saying nothing. For partners like these, I find it helpful to quickly model and then coach. For example, at one partnership you might listen to just a line or two and then jump in and say, "Oh wait, right there! I love that part when you talked about how the sun felt." Then turn to the listener and say, "Didn't you like that part, too? Quick, tell him to mark it so he doesn't forget which part we liked so much." Then say, "OK, writer, keep going. Your partner and I will listen for another good part. Ready, partner? You pick the next part." Then sit alongside to observe how the listener takes over. What you learn from partner interactions like these are important to record in your conference notes as an ongoing assessment of what your writers understand about writing (Anderson 2000; 2005).

In any stage of the writing process, these partnership conversations can help propel writers forward. For instance, while collecting is about helping students find powerful subjects they actually want to write about—and know their partners are interested in—revision is about helping your reader connect to your ideas. Nothing is more powerful than a peer saying, "Did you say anything to him? I would have. Maybe you should include that," to get a student off to revise.

As you develop more ways partners can support each other during the writing process, you might:

- Keep a chart for each stage in the writing process, suggesting ways partners can interact

- Think about what that stage of the process requires and what you do in your own writing
- Move around and coach conversations to teach strong and supportive communication

Value Their Need for Immediate Conversations: Create a Partner Spot

I know what you are thinking: not every student will patiently wait for "partner time" to begin. Sometimes they truly need help in order to continue with their writing; other times they need some variation during the period and benefit from a little physical movement. Therefore, you might designate a place in your classroom where partners can go to talk for a brief amount of time and with clear expectations. This "partner spot," or whatever name you and your class choose to call it, can accomplish several things. If you have an extra chatty class—all-around well meaning, just really chatty—it provides a way for you to both value their desire to communicate about their work while also putting clear parameters around when and where to converse. The partner spot also greatly supports your charge to develop independent thinkers and writers; it is a place in the room where writers can choose to go when they know they are in need of support and a place to try out their own ways of teaching and learning from one another.

To start, you do not need much of anything except a place in the room where students can easily meet while still being in eye contact with you and visible to other students—a small table or two desks pushed together or some beanbags in the corner work well. You want a spot that feels isolated enough that quiet conversations do not always disturb the same poor student nearby, though visible enough that you can easily monitor it without too much fuss. If you have a meeting space in your room, like a rug or mat, that might be a suitable place. Designate a portion of it in some way to make it feel all the more important and special.

You want to control traffic there and develop a sense in your partners of "getting right to it" and not wasting a moment of writing time. Adding an audible timing device, like an egg timer or digital timer, that you can hear when their time is over is important. You also want to make sure this place is for accountable conversations, so a simple sheet that has a place for partners to write their names, a few words about what they discussed, and an indication of where you could go to see evidence of the results of the conversation, usually is all you need. It might be a photocopied form or just a notebook where students learn to add the proper headings as they turn to a new page (see Figure 3.1).

Talking with Your Students

Like any other new feature in your room, take a few minutes to show your class how the partner spot works. You might introduce it like this:

(Describe the reason for the place in your room and really sell your students on the great opportunity you are providing them.)
"I just couldn't wait until you got to class today to show this to you. I'm so proud of how well you have been

Names	Purpose of Conference	Where Anyone Can See the Benefits of This Conversation and the Date
Chris and Dominique	I can't come up with any other ideas and I feel stuck	In my writer's notebook I tried a different strategy from the collecting chart, Sept 18

FIG. 3.1 *Sample Partner Spot Record Sheet*

supporting each other. So, I decided that you are ready to have a place in the room where you and your partner can choose to come, at any time, if you ever feel really stuck or want to get an idea or figure something out. I think you've earned this. I wouldn't trust just any class to have a responsibility like this."

(Teach the routines to your students, and give them an opportunity to practice at their seats.)

"So this spot over here is our new partner spot. Let me show you how it works. First, when you are sitting at your seat, if you become really stuck or really want to run an idea past your partner, you can ask him or her to come with you to this spot. If your partner says no, then you will have to move on with your work without a conversation, but if he or she says yes, then both of you can come here. The moment you sit down, set this timer on the table to two minutes. Then fill out this Partner Spot Record Sheet. Watch how I do it: first I'll write our names in this notebook where it says 'partners.'

"I'll put my name and Dominique is my pretend partner, so I'll write her name as well. Then writer, write down what you needed help with in the column that says, 'Purpose of the Conference' and tell your partner. So, I'll write, 'I can't come up with any other ideas and I feel stuck.' Then I'll tell my partner, 'Dominique, I feel really stuck. I've been writing for the first part of the period, but I feel like I ran out of ideas. I need help. I don't know what to do next.' Then you have until the timer goes off to get your partner's assistance. I'm going to see if Dominique has any ideas for me. Like, she probably will think about her own writing and what she does, and she will probably look around the room at charts that are up to help me. She might even ask me to read a little bit of what I wrote to her so she can get an idea about what I have been working on. Once the timer goes off, write what your solution is and where I could see the work that came from it in the last column, 'Where Anyone Can See the Benefits of This Conversation.' I'm going to do that part last, but first I want to give you a chance to help Dominique think of suggestions she could make. Turn to the person next to you and say, if you were Dominique, what could you say to me to help me get unstuck?"

(Give your class a chance to try out the role of the partner. While you listen in, remind them to look back to charts in the room and their own notebooks, and consider questions and suggestions they could share. Then report back what you heard and demonstrate how you would complete the guide sheet.)

"Wow. Lots of great suggestions! Some of you said I should look at the 'Collecting Writing Ideas' chart over by the clock and try one of them out. One pair said I should try the strategy out before the timer goes off, so that they could help me if I needed it. So, let's imagine I tried that out. Once the timer goes off I'll write in the last column, 'In my writer's notebook I tried a different strategy from the collecting chart' and then I'll put today's date."

Once your class starts using the partner spot, make it a point to check in on partners who are meeting and especially do some check-ins of the Partner Spot Record Sheet. For instance, you might bring the record sheet with you to a conference and say to the writer, "I noticed you wrote that you were having trouble on October 6 and asked your partner for help. You wrote here that you tried a new strategy from the chart, could you show me that so I can see how it went?" This gives you the opportunity to hold the student accountable, while also researching their use of the strategy, to see if there is anything you can teach that can assist them in the future.

When you add a partner spot to your classroom community, set procedures to keep it accountable and running well:

- ▶ Place the spot somewhere in the room that is clearly visible to both you and the class, so everyone knows when it is open or in use
- ▶ Set a standard amount of time for anyone using the partner spot: long enough to have a clear conversation, but short enough for it to be focused
- ▶ Follow up with students who use the spot, both while they are speaking and later in their writing

CHAPTER FOUR

Writers Who Constantly Ask If What They Are Doing Is Right

This chapter will help you to:

▶ Cut the codependence cord: allow for uncertainty, even model it

▶ Shine a light on your teaching: partner conferences can help you see transference

▶ Make chart paper, not wallpaper: teach into using supports in the room

Case Study

We teach our writers not only how to write but how to be. Sometimes we teach positive ways of being explicitly, but other times we inadvertently teach our students habits of mind which are, unfortunately, counter-productive to our desire to build independent writers and thinkers. This is often the case with our most struggling writers. One teacher in a New Jersey district coined her plight clearly. She, a special education teacher in an inclusion classroom, said that when it comes to the students with IEPs who are charged under her care, "I am a hovercraft. I can't help it. I just hover and hover and never let them be." Through the course of our conversation with her partner teacher and me she said, "I realize what I am doing to them. They expect me to be there and solve everything for them. It's not right, but I also am so worried about them."

She, like all of us, care so much about our students that we sometimes "over-coach" them, often to the point of doing all the thinking and struggling for them so that all they need to do is put their name on their paper and turn it back in. "Wow," we say, looking at their essays for grading. "Jonathan has come so far. Look at this great conclusion." I worry that so many of us, myself included, suffer from some short-term memory lapse condition. We forget the things that we co-authored in the hopes of "helping" and pat ourselves on the back for the one fish, well knowing that that student still has no idea how to hold a rod and reel.

In instances like the one the teacher described, my advice is to just leave them alone.

In one very high-performing classroom in Queens, New York, some teachers and I were in a gifted and talented sixth-grade class. I had just left a self-contained special education classroom, where we had been working on being "less hovercraft-ish" and allowing students to fiddle a bit on their own. Now, standing in front of a classroom of "high performers," I ended my lesson as usual, suggesting options for their work time and having them set a plan. No sooner did I say, "So turn to your partner and tell them what you plan to work on today," when five hands went up. Each one essentially asking, "So, you want us to do what you just did, right? You want us to make a chart just like that one, right?" I told them no, that they should decide what they, as writers, need to do today. My lesson was one option. A girl and her partner repeated, "OK, so make a plan to make the chart you made?"

I was struck by my own naivety, my own biases. I had believed that the struggle to write was mostly kept within our more struggling classrooms. I was so wrong. Everyone, even our "highest performers," can be disengaged writers. It seemed that these writers were teacher pleasers who could easily fill their pages with writing that appeared to be well thought and well crafted, when in actuality, many of them refused to be independent. Instead they needed to verify that every step they took was "right." Our youngest writers do this by standing up and following their teachers around the room, creating a tail of "Is this OK? Is this OK?" Our older writers can be much more elusive: sitting for long lengths of time, being "done" or doing nothing because they were unclear but do not want to ask you and appear foolish, or completing reams of paper that may rival the length of their classmates' work but actually took very little effort or thought to produce. We have to reinvent for these students what "doing it right" means.

Ways of Adjusting Your Teaching

Cut the Codependence Cord: Allow For Uncertainty, Even Model It

To reframe what "being a writer" means in our classrooms, we need to both talk and walk independent choices. We have to let our writers know that we actually do not want, maybe even cannot stand, when everyone is doing exactly what we just did in the minilesson. Because we, after all, are not mind readers; we could never possibly know what every single writer needs on every single day. If our writers do what we just did in the minilesson, then they are simply being puppets instead of thoughtful, engaged individuals. Though it is not enough to just say it, we have to live it, too. To stop hover-crafting, to cut the codependence cord, we need to stop jumping at the first cry-wolf calls, talk about the power of uncertainty, and make sure that our minilessons are not so "perfect" all the time.

My first bit of advice—and the behavior that teachers around the country always comment on when I work with their students—is this: if someone raises her hand, ignore it. There are different ways to finesse this, but that is basically the bottom line. Do not run when a hand goes up. I often approach this method in a few different ways. One is to literally not look. Your peripheral vision is a wonderful thing: when you see the hand, just keep walking and do not let the student know you saw her. Second, you might go over and say, "Do what you know you need to do as a writer. There is no right or wrong way. I'll come back in a few minutes to see what you tried." Then you may or may not return—I often do not. Third, you might help the student make a plan without getting too involved. I sometimes quickly say, "Use the room and use your notebook—find something that will help you keep writing." Then walk away. Walk away. Walk away.

When teachers talk with me after the class period they always say something like, "You didn't say anything to them, hardly. What if they were really stuck?" And I always end up saying back, "Did you see Rachael after? She first sat stunned for a little bit, but then she was writing lots and lots." And 98 percent of the time that is exactly what happens. Our disengaged writers often have little chance to problem-solve on their own because, in our wish to help them, we often take the struggle out of, well, struggle. Now, for the other 2 percent who, despite giving them space to think, really are overcome with feeling that they just cannot move on, we have to be proactive and experiment with other adjustments to our teaching, like making "mistakes" or "uncertainty" a force for good in your room, not a reason to shut down.

For example, another way to support student risk taking is to talk in minilessons or conferences about the power of uncertainty, how great ideas come from those moments when things do not feel easy and how even the greatest writers disengage with writing when they do not feel confident in their choices. In their book for poets on the craft of writing poetry, Kim Addonizio and Dorianne Laux (1997) devote a section to "self-doubt." In it they quote from Sylvia Plath's *Journals*, "Can I write? Will I write if I practice enough? How much should I sacrifice to writing anyway, before I find out if I'm any good?" It is astounding, yet also instructive, to see one of the most important poets and writers of our time be filled with a fear of not getting things quite right. And from what I know of other writers, this feeling is universal.

Consider this: because we are such careful planners, the writing we do during our minilessons nearly always goes well. If we want to model that we need more dialogue—boom, in moments we will have more well-crafted speech. If we want to model strong leads—bam, in seconds we have several to choose from. The real deal is that when we were planning those lessons we might have gone through multiple attempts, or spent time trying to figure out the best approach, or looking at professional texts, or even deleting some of what we wrote. We appear to be showing our students that with the tiniest bit of effort (in fact a brief minilesson's worth) writing just flows and flows. This, though, is entirely not true. Writing is not always easy; it is not always linear in a "I want this, so I do this" kind of way.

To help your writers see reflections of themselves in your demonstrations, you might consider bringing in a bit of the actual uncertainty you went through while planning. For example, as you prepare your demonstration writing, pay attention to what you actually do, then for some lessons you might weave in a bit of that uncertainty.

Talking with Your Students

While working on a lead during a demonstration, say, I might pause for a second and say something like this:

"OK, so I know my lead needs work, but now I'm not exactly sure what to even do. I could just sit here and do nothing, but that won't get me anywhere. Um . . . let me see, what could I do? Well, there's a chart on the wall over there about leads. What does that say? OK, I could start with dialogue, start with actions, start with setting. Hmmm . . . maybe I'll try a few and see which one I like the best."

The same could be done in a variety of other ways. For instance, you might be in the middle of teaching a lesson about revision, get confused, open up a section of a professional text, and say, "What was that great tip I read again? I know it was here somewhere. Oh! Here it is." Or if you have a partner spot set up in your room (see Chapter 3 for more on this), you can demonstrate smart things to say to a partner to help you get unstuck.

There is an art to this as well. You have to find the right balance between attempting to solve a problem and keeping your lesson focused. You might decide which days and which moments support this kind of modeling. Perhaps you would not do this during a tricky strategy that feels really new to your students. But you may show this tactic while demonstrating something you know feels familiar from previous years or one that you have already taught in this unit and are revisiting.

Some teachers I work with at first fear that this uncertainty makes them appear to be less than an expert, that it might tip the control differential in the room. Instead, what tends to happen is that students who naturally become disengaged tend to take on the same mannerisms that their teachers modeled while working through uncertainty. They begin to see uncertainty as a challenge that they are equipped and encouraged to take on.

To help your students be more independent
and rely on you less, you might:

- ▶ Avoid rushing to raised hands; instead ignore them or
  have them try to make a plan before you return later in
  the period
- ▶ Talk about how all writers, even famous ones, feel
  uncertain and how it is a moment of potential
- ▶ Make some lessons less "perfect"; plan to infuse some
  of your actual struggles

Shine a Light on Your Teaching: Partner Conferences Can Help You See Transference

One of our greatest concerns as teachers of writing revolves
around what our students are "getting" and "not getting." You
might sometimes overhear a colleague saying, "I feel like I
taught that lesson a million times and he's still not getting it!"

This is an issue of transference: how your students are able
(or not able) to take your teaching and transfer it into their
own practice. It is an essential element of building student
writing independence. However, it is also one that we, uncon-
sciously, often overlook. For your last five or six conferences
from this week, how many do you have a good sense of that
students will transfer what you taught into their own practice?
How many, if you are anything like me, do you feel you may
have guided too much or asked too many questions during,
and then walked away wondering if that student *really* "got"
your point. Or even in a conference that went particularly well,
are you certain of which points the writer understood and at

which points understanding may have started to break down for him?

This is where "partner conferences" can help a great deal. They can take many forms: perhaps you coach two students on the same issue and allow time to practice with both, or you conference with one student while another quietly watches. I want to suggest a third option. In order to see transference you can experiment with a conference in which you teach one student privately and then invite them to reteach your lesson to a peer.

Begin by holding a regular writing conference with one student. Perhaps start by researching what the student is doing and asking some questions, complimenting what she has done well to help her remember to do it again, and then teaching her something that can push her work as a writer a bit farther (Anderson 2000). This is the point where you might add a new method into your practice. At the end of the conference, ask the student to bring her partner over and "teach" that partner what you just taught her. Then you observe, looking for what transferred well and what did not.

Talking with Your Students

You might coach the writer to help him more clearly explain— and synthesize—what you taught him and also make note of what he understood from your teaching and what he did not:

(As you finish a conference with one student, have her bring her partner over to give you an opportunity to see if the writer can transfer your teaching.)

"You did such an amazing job! Look at how you went from a blank notebook page to so much writing all because you listed moments from your life for just a few seconds, then picked one, imagined you were there, and started writing. I'm so proud of you! I'm wondering, could you bring your partner over here and teach her how to do what you just did?"

[Partner comes over.]

"Hi, Mariama. Katie is going to teach you something she is getting really good at. She'll explain it to you and show you, and I might point out some things, too."

Katie begins, "So I made a list and then picked this one about my mom and then I wrote about it."

(As you listen, pay attention to what the student is transferring from your conference and what she is unclear about or missed completely. This might be a point where you want to jump back in and teach now or make note of for the future. More important, plan to reflect on why you think the point was unclear or forgotten.)

I coach, "Katie, can you show Mariama what you did? Use your notebook."

"Sure, so here is where I wrote the collecting list. Here is where I was writing about one of my ideas. I ended up writing way too much—this whole page and a half. So I stopped and went back and circled another idea and started writing about it here."

"That's great, Katie, can you go back and describe how you started the new entry? Remember what I did in mine?"

Katie continues to teach, "Oh yeah, when I started writing, I closed my eyes and tried to imagine where I was, then I started to write the moment. See, like right here . . ."

From an interaction like this I learn several things about the writer and about myself. I learn that I should follow up with her in our next few conferences on trying to picture a scene before writing about it, because when she was talking she needed me to coach her a little to remind her of that strategy. I also learned that in my teaching I need to be clearer when a strategy has multiple steps because it seemed hard for her to hold onto each part of what I taught her. Maybe next time I should count the steps on my fingers or have the student jot them down. I also realize I am thinking more about ways of making my teaching more memorable—was there a catchy phrase I could have used or a chart I could have pointed to or something I could have had her write or mark in front of me?

Having two students involved in your conference helps you see how your disengaged writers are interacting with and using your teaching. Our disengaged writers, and particularly those who are always asking if what they are doing is "right" or "good," are sometimes not understanding the whole picture of our lessons and conferences. Noticing transference helps us to see what ideas our students have gleaned from our instruction and ways we can support them better in the future through our own revised methods.

As you experiment more with ways partner conferences can help you notice transference, keep these points in mind:

- Start with one student, then invite a second in at the end
- As one student "teaches" the other, be a silent researcher; jot down where and when the writer is in sync or out of sync with the intent of your conference

- Reflect on your teaching practice: notice patterns across time with one student, and patterns across several students and adjust your methods accordingly

Make Chart Paper, Not Wallpaper: Teach into Using Supports in the Room

In *On Writing*, the prolific suspense writer Steven King talks about constructing a writer's toolbox: "I want to suggest that to write to your best abilities, it behooves you to construct your own toolbox and then build up enough muscle so you can carry it with you. Then, instead of looking at a hard job and getting discouraged, you will perhaps seize the correct tool and get immediately to work." For our middle school students, this toolbox can start as the walls of our classroom.

To help our disengaged writers take on more responsibility for their own decisions we can make our classrooms as supportive as possible. An assistant principal I work with in Queens, New York, talks with his staff about the room having "silent teachers": charts, notes, references that teach our students while remaining unassuming off to the side. I love that analogy. As I think about the kinds of "silent teachers" in classrooms I visit, it makes me think how those large pieces of paper taped to the wall really do need to be as planned, engaging, and accessible as any other instruction we perform. This means a few things.

One, we have to have them organized in a way that makes them feel like a reference book. If an encyclopedia were randomly thrown together in any fashion—an article about gorillas here, followed by some drawing of Saturn, followed immediately by an illegible list of car models—no one would use them. Instead, you know that if you pick up an encyclopedia labeled "Volume J–K," you will find articles on jazz and kangaroos and each will have headings, pictures, and descriptions—and you know you'll get condensed information quickly.

Charts, notebooks, and reference materials should feel the same way. Our students should know how to use our charts and that the charts should generally work in similar ways. They should know where in the room writing charts are and where reading charts are. Perhaps they know that instead of alphabetically they are organized by the steps of the writing process or by kinds of writing. They should know what the titles mean. Perhaps the charts should contain some graphics. Probably there should be enough words to figure out what is going on, but not so many that it takes half the period to get through reading just one, much less using it. Dictionaries should probably be in a section that makes sense, perhaps even near your editing charts. Mentor texts should be really easy to find in your library or near the area you demonstrate in.

Second, the downside of these extra teachers being "silent" is that they can actually start to fade into the background. Our charts, notebooks, and mentor texts can simply become wallpaper. To avoid this, we have to make them a part of our regular demonstrations. Earlier in this chapter I described a lesson in which I modeled trying to deal with uncertainty by using a chart in the room. I did three things with that brief demonstration. I first modeled feeling stuck and I thought out loud, "How can I figure out what to do?" Next, I looked to a chart, read it, and considered solutions. Last, I showed how I used the information on the chart to help me.

While modeling for a class, I could add in almost anything a student usually says to me in order to tailor the lesson toward them. For instance, in place of "How can I figure out what to do?" I could have said, "Is this right? Am I doing what I think I'm supposed to be doing? Let me see if there is something in the room I could check." I can show students how the resources in our classroom can help them with their specific needs.

Last, we need to make accessing supports in the room a part of our students' regular practice. You could do this during conferences, during times that partners or small groups work together, or as students make plans for the period or plans for homework.

Talking with Your Students

Near the end of the period, when partners are talking to one another about their writing, I might sometimes say something like:

> *(Connect the resources in the room to what students have been working on. Have them interact with the resources in some way to remind them of their use.)*
>
> "We've been working a lot on revisions this week. Would you take just a moment with your partner and look over our revision charts? Then, would you use your finger and kind of

check off in the air all the strategies you've tried. Tell your partner which ones you're checking as you do it. Then, you might even talk about which ones you haven't tried—or maybe even forgot about—that you think you want to experiment with soon."

This exercise generally leads to a combination of students realizing there are a lot of things they have been trying in their writing, as well as noticing some things that they have not tried yet. Whatever opportunities you take for this sort of check in, it is important that we make our charts and other references usable and have our students engage with them regularly.

Sometimes the question arises whether it is even necessary to use chart paper with middle schoolers. After all, shouldn't they just remember these things? I am not adverse to imagining other ways to support students in referencing prior teaching. A great seventh-grade team I work with in New Jersey makes small PowerPoint printouts of important charts for their students that they can glue right into writing notebooks. I, however, do think about my own busy life: when I have something important to do that I do not want to forget about, I make a list and post it somewhere visible. I find charts in older classrooms can feel as age appropriate as you choose to make them. In addition, they not only remind students of your teaching but can be a great reference for you, too.

Plus, when a student says, "Is this right?" you can just whiz quickly by and say, "Well, check the chart."

As you teach into the supports in your classroom,
you might try a few things:

- Treat your charts and materials like a reference book:
  have them organized in a way that is easy and
  predictable to use
- Model yourself using the resources in the room
- Have students interact with them across the day and
  across the unit, so they do not fade into the
  background

CHAPTER FIVE

Devising Your Own Responses to Disengagement

I hope the methods from the first four chapters give you great traction with your disengaged writers. I also know, though, that as each new September comes around you will be faced with a few different challenges from the year before. This chapter describes one way that you, and perhaps some colleagues, can conduct an inquiry into disengaged writers and devise your own responses.

Researching Your Own Disengaged Middle School Writers

Collecting Information to Inform Your Approach

A basic belief I hold about not just the teaching of writing but about teaching in general is that students thrive the most in our classrooms when they feel safe and when they feel smart. If they feel safe—not threatened by a bully, not anxious that they might be humiliated or put on the spot, and, of course, not dealing with the threat or reality of some form of abuse—and if they feel smart—not faced with a task they repeatedly "fail" at, not believing they're "dumb" because their own strengths are not put into use, and not placed in situations where they are compared to others—our students are less inclined to react negatively or avoid the task at hand. Resiliency studies document what we already intuit to be true: "Adolescents with higher levels of self-confidence relied more on coping strategies directed at *solving the problem*, whereas those who selected *avoidance* strategies demonstrated less self-confidence" (italics added, Moos 1990, as referenced in Chapman 1999). Essentially, when our disengaged writers feel confident and supported they are less likely to avoid tasks, to argue with us, or to take on a larger than life persona in order to hide their real fears and self-perceived deficiencies.

What drew me to workshop teaching, and why I became so enamored with it, was that I felt that woven within the fabric of a writing workshop is the belief that all of us, of all ages, are writers at heart and that every one of our lives is worth writing about (Calkins and Martinelli 2006). The methods and structures of workshop teaching allow me time to carefully reflect on the needs of my students at all levels of proficiency, to plan teaching that supports individuals and the group, and to build independence, courage, and strength in each middle school writer, at a time in their lives when most of them are not feeling so independent, courageous, or strong. Workshop, for me, was a place where my students could feel safe and smart and could really thrive.

Therefore, I want my investigation into my disengaged writers to carry that same tone and guiding principals. I choose to not go into this inquiry trying to "figure out what's wrong" *with them*; instead I observe their actions and then try to decipher what is missing in *my teaching*. This is not to say that I doubt my—or your—ability to teach; it is just the opposite. I believe that I—like you—am confident in my ability to adjust my methods and my approach, that I am willing to look at situations in my classroom knowing that it is *my work* that needs to change. I believe that with a little support I can do just that.

What follows is one process I have used alongside teams of teachers to develop many of the ideas found in this book. First, watch your students' actions and record what you notice with as little judgment as possible. Then, look across what you have gathered for patterns and create a theory about the student or students. Finally, decide how to take action by adjusting your teaching.

Step One: Observing and Gathering

When troubles arise, I suggest you first turn to the response of all professional fields, be it your family doctor determining why you have a cough or your mechanic uncovering the cause of that rattle that just started under the hood: you open your eyes wide, your ears even wider, go to the problem and do a little research to try to figure out the cause.

Plan that for a few days you will watch your classroom or perhaps partner with a colleague and watch her class before she comes to watch yours. Pay attention in particular to students who often disengage with writing. You might decide that you wish to take mental notes because they feel quicker and easier to gather. However, with everything that we have to keep our minds on across a day—both in school and out—mental notes can get murky and you may instead decide to make some pen and paper jottings, even quickly, to both hold you to the task at hand while also providing an easier way for you and your colleagues to look for patterns. As you jot your thinking, try to remain unbiased and record events as they happen. Think of yourself as a scientist recording notes in the field (see Figure 5.1).

As you observe you might organize your notes around a few key questions:

- ❯ At what points in the period do students (or a key student) disengage and, conversely, at what points do they appear the most engaged? *During a certain point of the minilesson? At the start of independent work time? In the middle? At the end? Before a conference? During a conference? After the conference? On days when the strategy is familiar? With narrative writing? With essay writing? During a particular point in the writing process?*

- ❯ What are the students' (or student's) actions during points of disengagement? *What specific things are they doing? Stopping their writing? Continuing their writing? What are they writing? Asking to leave the room? Talking to someone else? What are they talking about?*

Student Name(s): Sean		Class: 702	

Dates Planning to Observe: Mon 2nd, Wed 4th, and Thurs 5th   .

Ongoing Record of Times When an Action Was Noticed	Engaged or Disengaged?	Event in Class	Specific Action of Student
Monday, 8:05AM	E	minilesson	Sitting quietly, looking forward, nodding
	E	active involvement of the lesson	Really spoke well with his partner, Mario; had good ideas for my writing demo piece
8:18AM	D	beginning of work-time	Tapping pencil, looking around room, trying to catch John's eye
8:25AM	D	worktime	Wrote a few lines but no more. Talked to John (ignored), talked to Mario who listened; couldn't hear what he said to him
8:32AM	E	midworkshop interruption	Spoke well with John when everyone asked to talk briefly; gave good suggestion about John's lead
8:45AM	E/D	worktime	Wrote half page after talking with John, but then put pencil down and tried to get Mario's attention again
Tuesday, 8:05AM	E	minilesson	Listening actively, looks interested

FIG. 5.1 *A Way You Might Organize Observation Notes*

- What are the students' (or student's) actions during points of engagement? *Talking with others? With you? What are they talking about? Writing quietly alone? What are they writing about?*

- Plan to record observations for the same student(s) on a few pre-determined days. They need not be consecutive, but they should allow you to see the writer across more than one day. Be sure to plan for this just as you would any other important meeting or deadline so that daily classroom life does not sneak up and rob you of your research time!

Step Two: Look for Patterns and Develop a Theory

Once you have gathered a few days worth of observations, look across your notes—and the notes of your colleagues if they joined you—and look for patterns. You might notice an individual student or group generally begins to talk when they are disengaged and that disengagement usually happens right after the lesson. Or maybe you notice a student who is more engaged during collecting but fades away during rehearsal of her ideas. Or maybe a student is constantly asking for your feedback but quickly loses focus when you are not with him. Again, just as in observing, try to hold your preconceptions about that student to the side; otherwise you might tend to immediately see what you already wanted to. For example, you may find yourself jumping forward to say, "Yep, he's really needy. He can't do anything without me by himself," whereas if you hold back judgment and consider all patterns, you might instead realize that he is not focused when he feels he has completed an entry and has not yet internalized a way to move himself to the next bit of work.

As you look across the data you gathered
you might consider a few patterns:

- ▶ Time: a repeated moment during the period when the students disengage

- ▶ Action: a repeated behavior (talking, tapping, calling for you, and so on) that the students use when they disengage

- ▶ Response: a repeated response from you or a peer during the disengagement (you go to them, their peer starts talking, and so on)

- ▶ Product: a repeated type or level of work that results from disengagement

After gathering patterns, you can then create a theory about the behavior. It seems essential to consider several possible theories, or perhaps say "or maybe" a few times as you consider the cause. For example, you might say, "I think Julia disengages because she isn't sure what to do next or maybe it is because she needs help making a plan or maybe it is because . . ." This is another perfect opportunity for a conversation with your colleagues, examining the collected observations and then sharing your theories.

Step Three: Devise How You Will Adjust Your Teaching

I was about to write "I have worked with *many* teachers who have disengaged students," but I stopped myself, realizing that we *all* have some students who fit this bill. And we *all* know how much steam we lose every time Jason gets out of his seat or Chandra talks throughout the whole class period. If you go into this study thinking that one day of adjustment will change the world, then you are mistaken. Instead you have to decide how to approach the theories you have developed and then commit to a short-term plan.

Once you have arrived at a theory, it is time to build this short-term plan of action. This is the moment where you become a bit like a personal trainer. Set a short, achievable goal, with a realistic time frame, and then hold yourself and your student to it. If you aspire to lose twenty pounds, you know you have to stick with a program for the long haul—one day of sweating on a treadmill will not do it—but you also know that if you tell yourself "I'll lose twenty pounds in six months" and you put on a few pounds at any point in those six months you will probably lose faith and stop. Instead you know that you need to say, "I'll lose two pounds this week," so that you feel a little success that keeps you going. Same goes for supporting our disengaged writers.

One example might look like this: you might have studied Chandra with your colleagues and together you noticed that she is most disengaged when she feels uncertain of what to do to make her writing better. You noticed that she then usually turns to Samantha and tries to engage her in a conversation. Your theory might be that Chandra relies on others to keep her going because she cannot see her strengths or options of what to do herself.

You and your colleagues might then page through this book for ideas and look to, say, Chapter 3 on students who talk too much during writing time and Chapter 4 on students who are not confident and always ask for help, and then develop some of your own ideas, building off of structures and methods presented here. You then might decide to start small. You might choose just one or two ways to adjust your teaching as a start, perhaps deciding to create a partner spot in your room or making resources in your room more supportive for your students.

With your colleagues, or alone, make a short-term, specific plan with a reasonable time frame. It helps to write it down somewhere and get others involved. It could go like this:

(When you jot down your short-term plan, start with your time frame and what specific adjustment to your teaching you are trying to make.)

"For the next two weeks I will establish a partner spot in the room."

(Explain the steps you will take and who will be involved in helping you and the students keep to those steps.)

"I am going to introduce it to my classes on Monday and then I am going to pick one responsible student in each class to remind me after the minilesson each day to check the log. I will try to encourage one or two partnerships every day to go over, instead of getting angry right away when they want to talk. I want to try and get Chandra over to the spot with Samantha a few times and see if she will start to go on her own. The log should show how it's going."

(Plan how you will check in on your progress and reflect on its effectiveness and decide what next steps need to be taken.)

"At the end of two weeks I'll bring the log back to our grade level meeting to share how it went. I will also ask my classes what they think. My next goal will then be to work on supportive resources in the room, but I won't try that until later."

Notice how this goal is small enough and has enough people involved with it that it feels very possible to achieve. It is short term—you are not doing it alone—and you will bring back artifacts to share, which ultimately holds you to it. Most important, know that there will be bumps in the road. You might lose it one day—just like you might eat that extra piece of cake during your exercise routine—but in the end know that you are completely in control of what you do in the classroom, so you can always readjust and keep studying your students and yourself.

Closing Thoughts on Reviving Our Disengaged Writers

Though challenging, our disengaged writers provide us an opportunity to refine our teaching and learn more about our practice in general. When we commit to observing them, making short-term plans to support them, and experimenting with adjustments in our own teaching, we are doing just what we set out to do when we first decided to become teachers. We are creating possibilities and opportunities for our writers and for their lives.

As your year moves from one month to the next, remember a few things you have been trying during our work together:

Observe your students.

Watch both your disengaged student (or students) as well as those who are connecting with writing. These observations, as discussed in this chapter, can help you better describe the issue and make a short-term plan.

Look to professional books.

Look for books that speak to the struggles you are facing as well as more general writing topics that you can lift ideas from. M. Colleen Cruz's *A Quick Guide to Reaching Struggling Writers, K–5* (2008) can help with a variety of issues of our most struggling writers, including those with physical writing issues, like pencil grip, to those who struggle with spelling. Or Chantal Francois and Elisa Zonana's *Catching Up On Conventions: Grammar Lessons For Middle School Writers* (2009), which details the authors' attempts at revising their grammar instruction and the practical structures they discovered.

Talk with your colleagues.

There is no better way to revise your teaching than to work closely with your peers. It is my daily work, studying with groups of teachers as well as working closely with my own colleagues back at our organization. Having multiple eyes on a problem raises issues and opportunities you never see alone. In my experience, the schools that grow the most and most support their students are those that are having the most professional conversations.

Observe yourself.

If students are struggling with something, get into their shoes and try doing what you are asking them to try. Use the same strategy or write the same piece. Notice moments when you disengage, have trouble, or need to think in a new way. Equally, pay attention to your methods and how your students respond to them.

Disengagement is just one of the many challenges you face each year in your writing workshop. Your commitment to continually adjusting your teaching in response to the needs of your students is not only brave, is not only admirable, but is the greatest gift you can give your writers.

WORKS CITED

Addonizio, K. and Laux, D. 1997. *The Poet's Companion: A Guide to the Pleasures of Writing Poetry.* New York: W. W. Norton and Company.

Anderson, C. 2000. *How's It Going: A Practical Guide to Conferring with Student Writers.* Portsmouth, NH: Heinemann.

————. 2005. *Assessing Writers.* Portsmouth, NH: Heinemann.

Booth, D. 2009. *I Am the Book! When Children Find Themselves Inside the Texts They Are Reading.* Speech presented at Teachers College, Columbia University, New York, NY.

Calkins, L. M. 1994. *The Art of Teaching Writing.* Portsmouth, NH: Heinemann.

Calkins, L. and Martinelli, M. 2006. *Launching the Writing Workshop.* Portsmouth, NH: Heinemann.

Chapman, P. and Mullis, R. 1999. Adolescent Coping Strategies and Self-Esteem. *Child Study Journal, 29*(1), 69.

Cruz, M. C. 2008. *A Quick Guide to Reaching Struggling Writers, K–5.* Portsmouth, NH: Heinemann.

Ehrenworth, M. and Vinton, V. 2005. *The Power of Grammar: Unconventional Approaches to the Conventions of Language.* Portsmouth, NH: Heinemann.

Elbow, P. 1998. *Writing Without Teachers.* New York: Oxford University Press, USA.

Francois, C. and Zonana, E. 2009. *Catching Up on Conventions: Grammar Lessons for Middle School Writers.* Portsmouth, NH: Heinemann.

Graves, D. 1983. *Writing: Teachers and Children at Work.* Exeter, NH: Heinemann Educational Books.

Johnson, A. 2004. *The First Part Last.* New York: Simon Pulse.

Johnston, P. H. 2004. *Choice Words: How Our Language Affects Children's Learning.* Portland, ME: Stenhouse Publishers.

King, S. 2000. *On Writing: A Memoir of the Craft.* New York: Pocket Books.

Meyer, S. 2006. *Twilight: The Twilight Saga, Book 1.* New York: Little, Brown Young Readers.

Ray, Katie Wood. 1999. *Wondrous Words: Writers and Writing in the Elementary Classroom.* Urbana, IL: National Council of Teachers of English.

Riordan, R. 2006. *The Lightning Thief: Percy Jackson and the Olympians, Book 1.* New York: Miramax.

Santman, D. 2005. *Shades of Meaning: Comprehension and Interpretation in Middle School.* Portsmouth, NH: Heinemann.

Zinsser, W. 2006. *On Writing Well: The Classic Guide to Writing Nonfiction* (30th anniversary edition). New York: Harper Paperbacks.

Consider these other books in the

A Quick Guide to Teaching Persuasive Writing, K–2

Children have voices that need to be heard and ideas that need to be understood. Building on this premise **Sarah Picard Taylor** describes why you should try a persuasive writing unit of study, describes two units of study for the primary classroom, and lists tips and ideas for helping students get their persuasive writing out into the world.

Grades K–2 / 978-0-325-02597-1 / 2008 / 96pp / $8.00

A Quick Guide to Boosting English Acquisition in Choice Time, K–2

Cheryl Tyler and **Alison Porcelli** explain how choice-time workshops can be structured to help English language learners imagine, create, and explore language through play. They outline two units of study for choice-time workshops, the first using open-ended materials, the other using literature to inspire play.

Grades K–2 / 978-0-325-02615-2 / 2008 / 96pp / $8.00

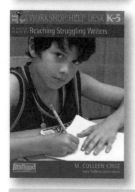

A Quick Guide to Reaching Struggling Writers, K–5

Colleen Cruz shows how to stop struggling with writers who struggle. You'll find effective support for students who say: *I'm not a good writer; My hand hurts; I don't know how to spell; I don't have anything to write about; I never get to write anything I want to write; I'm done.*

Grades K–5 / 978-0-325-02595-7 / 2008 / 96pp / $8.00

Pocket-sized professional development on topics of interest to you.